# MRS FARNSWORTH

## *A R Gurney*

**BROADWAY PLAY PUBLISHING INC**
56 E 81st St., NY NY 10028-0202
212 772-8334  fax: 212 772-8358
http://www.BroadwayPlayPubl.com

MRS FARNSWORTH
© Copyright 2004 by A R Gurney

For all rights contact Peter Franklin, William Morris Agency, 1325 6th Ave, New York, NY 10019, 212-903-1550.

First printing: April 2004
Second printing: February 2005
I S B N: 0-88145-237-8

Book design: Marie Donovan
Word processing: Microsoft Word for Windows
Typographic controls: Xerox Ventura Publisher 2.0 P E
Typeface: Palatino
Printed and bound in the U S A

# ABOUT THE AUTHOR

A R Gurney has written many plays. Among them are:
SCENES FROM AMERICAN LIFE, THE DINING
ROOM, THE COCKTAIL HOUR, LOVE LETTERS,
LATER LIFE, SYLVIA, FAR EAST, ANCESTRAL
VOICES and BIG BILL. He has also written several
novels, a few television scripts, and the libretto of
STRAWBERRY FIELDS, a one-act opera. He has
received a number of awards including ones from
the Drama Desk, the National Endowment of the Arts,
the Rockefeller Foundation, The American Academy
and Institute of Arts and Letters, and a Lucille Lortel
Award for the body of his work. He has honorary
degrees from Williams College and Buffalo State
College S U N Y, and taught literature at M I T for
many years before committing himself to full-time
writing.

MRS FARNSWORTH was first produced at the
Flea Theater in New York City (Jim Simpson, Artistic
Director; Carol Ostrow, Producing Director) The play
opened on 7 April 2004, with the following cast and
creative contributors:

GORDON . . . . . . . . . . . . . . . . . . . . . . . . Danny Burstein
AMY NEEDLEMAN . . . . . . . . . . . . . . . . . . . . Kate Benson
MRS FARNSWORTH . . . . . . . . . . . . . . . Sigourney Weaver
MR FARNSWORTH . . . . . . . . . . . . . . . . . . John Lithgow
RICK COSTELLO . . . . . . . . . . . . . . Fernando Gambaroni
JANET SANCHEZ . . . . . . . . . . . . . . . . . . Tarajia Morrell

*Director* . . . . . . . . . . . . . . . . . . . . . . . . . . . . . Jim Simpson
*Set* . . . . . . . . . . . . . . . . . . . . . . . . . . . . . . . Kyle Chepulis
*Lighting* . . . . . . . . . . . . . . . . . . . . . . . . . . . . Brian Aldous
*Costumes* . . . . . . . . . . . . . . . . . . . . . . . . . Claudia Brown
*Production stage manager* . . . . . . . . . Jennifer Noterman

# CHARACTERS & SETTING

GORDON BELL, *youngish, a part-time instructor of writing at a university in Manhattan*
MRS FARNSWORTH, *middle-aged, a suburban matron*
FORREST FARNSWORTH, *middle-aged, her husband*
AMY NEEDLEMAN, *a student*
RICK COSTELLO, *a student*
JANET SANCHEZ, *a student*

*The entire play takes place in a classroom on an upper floor of a a university building in downtown Manhattan on a weekday evening in early 2004. The stage is the instructor's area at the front of the class, consisting of an old wooden table or desk, several battered wooden chairs, and a chalk board behind. On the chalk board, there are faint, under-erased echoes of earlier courses taught in this room. Also there might be a dusty window or two upstage, through which we might see a skyline of the city at night, and because of which we are reminded that we're on an upper floor. There also might be a practical clock on the wall indicating real time. For example, if the play starts at 8 P M, the clock says so. The audience, of course, is the class and there should be no intermission.*

for Sigourney Weaver

*(At rise)*

*(No one is on stage. Then a loud school buzzer is heard.*
GORDON *enters through the audience. He is in his thirties,*
*an instructor of writing, and rather scruffily dressed. He*
*carries a backpack which he tosses onto the table. He goes to*
*the blackboard and writes "MRS FARNSWORTH.")*

GORDON: *(To audience)* Is Mrs Farnsworth here?
*(Indicating the board)* I am putting names on the board
so that we all can begin to connect names with faces...
Hence: Mrs Farnsworth. *(A moment)* So...Mrs
Farnsworth? ...What? No Mrs Farnsworth? *(He takes out*
*small piece of blue note-paper. It is monogrammed, with neat,*
*round writing in blue ink on it.)* I received this letter in the
mail from Mrs Farnsworth. She writes me this special
note... *(Reading)* "May I please go first tonight?" she
writes. And then she's a no-show. Hmmm. Well.
Onward and upward. *(Looks at class)* Who else is
on deck? I remember a request from one Amy
Needleman.... *(Writes "AMY NEEDLEMAN" on the*
*board, turns to audience)* May we assume that Amy
Needleman is here?

AMY: *(Who is seated in a rear row of the audience)* I'm here.

GORDON: Then there is a God.... You have something to
read to us, Amy?

AMY: I have a poem about my cat.

GORDON: Come up and read it.

AMY: O K.

(AMY *starts for the stage. A woman's voice is heard from the back*)

MRS FARNSWORTH: Wait!

GORDON: Who's that?

MRS FARNSWORTH: I'm Mrs Farnsworth.

GORDON: Ah hah!

(MRS FARNSWORTH *appears. She is pretty, middle-aged, well dressed, and carries an expensive-looking tote bag.*)

GORDON: Amy, do you think your cat would mind waiting until after Mrs Farnsworth?

AMY: That's cool.

GORDON: *(Indicating the note)* Because Mrs Farnsworth wrote this note.

(AMY *huffily returns to her seat.*)

MRS FARNSWORTH: I hope I'm not being grabby.

GORDON: No, no. Consider yourself at bat, Mrs Farnsworth.

MRS FARNSWORTH: Thank you. *(Breathlessly)* I'm terribly sorry. My train was late. And when I got to Grand Central, it was impossible to get a cab. I finally jumped on the subway and ran practically all the way from the 4th street station. *(She holds out her hand to* GORDON.*)* Hi.

(*They shake hands.*)

GORDON: So you're Mrs Farnsworth.

MRS FARNSWORTH: That's what I keep telling myself.

GORDON: *(Indicating)* I put it on the board so we'll all know who you are.

MRS FARNSWORTH: Good idea.

GORDON: *(Looking at note)* Your first name is Margery, I see.

MRS FARNSWORTH: Last time I looked.

GORDON: Mind if we call you that?

MRS FARNSWORTH: Margery? Oh. Well. All right.

GORDON: I sense some hesitation.

MRS FARNSWORTH: Oh no.

GORDON: Oh yes.

MRS FARNSWORTH: Well look, here's the thing. I had this grandmother who thought there was too much first-naming in this country. She said it destroyed personal distances.

GORDON: Nothing wrong with that.

MRS FARNSWORTH: There was to her. She said the world worked better when people knew where they stood. She had definite rules about that.

GORDON: Rules?

MRS FARNSWORTH: Rules.

GORDON: Such as?

MRS FARNSWORTH: Such as never let people call you by your first name if they work for you. Or if you've known them for less than three years. Or if you've never kissed them.

GORDON: We'll call you Mrs Farnsworth.

MRS FARNSWORTH: It's just that I'm used to it. When these strangers call up on the telephone, and use my first name, I hang up immediately.

GORDON: Gotcha. Besides, it will be easier to remember. You seem like a Mrs Farnsworth to me.

MRS FARNSWORTH: Is that good or bad?

GORDON: We'll soon find out.

MRS FARNSWORTH: I apologize for being late, by the way. That damn train.

GORDON: I take it you commute.

MRS FARNSWORTH: Just for this class.

GORDON: Where from?

MRS FARNSWORTH: You don't want to know.

GORDON: I do, I do.

MRS FARNSWORTH: Then I don't want to tell you. Because it will prejudice you against me.

GORDON: Oh come on.

MRS FARNSWORTH: I come from New Canaan, Connecticut.

GORDON: That's near Greenwich, isn't it?

MRS FARNSWORTH: *(To audience)* See? Here we go. Here comes some crack about Greenwich...

GORDON: Not from me.

MRS FARNSWORTH: People think Greenwich is full of rich Republicans.

GORDON: Isn't it?

MRS FARNSWORTH: Oh it is. But New Canaan's very different.

GORDON: I take it you're not a rich Republican.

MRS FARNSWORTH: Not on your life! I'm a rich Democrat.

GORDON: Ah hah.

MRS FARNSWORTH: And I signed up for this course because I know you're a Democrat, too.

GORDON: How'd you know that?

MRS FARNSWORTH: I read your poem in *The Nation.*

GORDON: Did you like it?

MRS FARNSWORTH: I did. I liked the fact that you're very angry about what's going on in our country these days.

GORDON: I am, I am.

MRS FARNSWORTH: Well guess what. So am I. Which is why I want to go first.

GORDON: You've written something political, Mrs Farnsworth?

MRS FARNSWORTH: I believe I have.

GORDON: These days it's hard to write anything else.

MRS FARNSWORTH: Exactly! And with an election right around the corner, it's time to speak out..

GORDON: I'll buy that.

MRS FARNSWORTH: I mean, there are political issues everywhere you look. Take tonight, for example. The reason my train was delayed is because of faulty switching equipment. And the reason for that is because the Republicans have systematically neglected public transportation.

GORDON: Sounds like you're ready to read us your piece, Mrs Farnsworth.

MRS FARNSWORTH: I am indeed. *(Puts her bag on the desk, begins to open it)*

GORDON: Is there anything you'd like us to know before you start?

MRS FARNSWORTH: *(Groping in her bag)* Let's just let the chips fall where they may.

GORDON: Is this a poem, or a short story, or what?

MRS FARNSWORTH: It's a book.

GORDON: A book?

MRS FARNSWORTH: *(Still rummaging)* If I can *find* it.

GORDON: You intend to read us a whole book, Mrs Farnsworth?

MRS FARNSWORTH: Heavens no! I'm not *that* dumb. I just plan to read the first paragraph.

GORDON: Oh. O K.

MRS FARNSWORTH: And from the progress I'm making in this purse you'll be lucky to get even that. *(More to herself)* Do you suppose I could have left the damn thing home? *(To audience)* I think Freud may have something to tell us here.

GORDON: Is it fact or fiction? *(He writes "FACT VS FICTION" on the board.)*

MRS FARNSWORTH: I suppose you could say it's a little of both.

GORDON: *(To audience)* As most writing is.

MRS FARNSWORTH: Though this particular masterpiece may tilt rather dangerously toward—well, what do you know? *(To audience)* Eureka! *(She waves a piece of paper.)* Hiding away among the flotsam and jetsam of my life!

GORDON: That is your book?

MRS FARNSWORTH: The first paragraph of my book.

GORDON: *(Placing a chair)* Would you like to sit down while you read it?

MRS FARNSWORTH: I would not.

GORDON: You prefer to stand?

MRS FARNSWORTH: I do. And I'll tell you why. My grandmother used to say.... *(To audience)* Or am I boring you with my grandmother?

GORDON: No, no.

MRS FARNSWORTH: I adored her, you know.

GORDON: We gathered that.

MRS FARNSWORTH: My grandmother used to say.... Promise you won't make a crack about her, after you hear this.

GORDON: Scout's honor.

MRS FARNSWORTH: My grandmother used to say that Americans like to sit down too much. *(More to audience)* We're always sitting around, she'd say. Standing up is good for you, especially if you stand up straight. Always stand up after meals, for example. It helps the digestion. And if you have to stand in line—at the butcher's, maybe, or cashing a check at a bank—always do some exercise. Practice tightening the muscles in your rear end, for example. It keeps you in shape.

GORDON: You might tell that to folks waiting in line for their unemployment checks.

MRS FARNSWORTH: Knew it! A crack!

GORDON: I couldn't help it.

MRS FARNSWORTH: Oh well, I suppose she asked for it, my grandmother. But I think she was onto something. She sensed that we were all fast becoming a bunch of fat slobs, and dammit, we are! Slouching over the steering wheels of those huge, hulking S U Vs, depending on elevators when we could easily use the stairs, eating those greasy pizzas when we could just as well make a cool, simple salad.

GORDON: Maybe you should begin reading.

MRS FARNSWORTH: Absolutely—if I can just find my glasses. *(More rummaging) Voici! (Holds them up)* O K. Ready or not, here I come. *(Puts on her glasses, begins to read, hesitantly at first, gaining confidence as SHE goes along)* "When I was at Vassar in the late 1960's, we used to go skiing during spring vacation. A group of us girls would pile into a car, and off we'd go to Vermont—Stowe, or Mad River, or Bromley, depending on the snow conditions and whether we could find a place to stay. And, of course, there were always the boys. We'd get onto the slopes, and there they'd be—boys we might have sailed with over the summer, or met at some football game in the fall, or danced with at some of the Christmas get-togethers. Boys who had draft deferments from the Viet Nam war because they were still in college. They'd have driven up from Williams or Yale or Princeton, and before long we'd be riding up on the chair-lift with them, or following them down the trickier trails, or meeting them afterwards at Smuggler's Notch or Johnny See-Saw's for a round of beer and a bowl of chili con carne. And because this was spring, there would be plenty of sun, so you could get a terrific tan. And by midday you'd be taking off your parka at the top of the lift, and handing it to the attendant, who'd send it back down on an empty chair, and you'd find it waiting for you at the bottom. I don't remember anyone ever having a parka stolen, either. So you see there was a common sense of trust at that time. And if a strange boy asked you to ski with him, there was a good chance that you knew someone he knew, so you could trust him, too. And if you slept with him that night—because that could happen, too, you know, even back then, once in a while, if the circumstances were right—you could trust him not to tell about it. It was a world of trust, up and down the line." *(Pause. She looks up from her reading, takes off her glasses.)*

GORDON: That's it?

MRS FARNSWORTH: That's it.

GORDON: It's a beginning.

MRS FARNSWORTH: Don't they say "well begun is half done"?

GORDON: I'll bet your grandmother said that.

MRS FARNSWORTH: Actually she did.

GORDON: Though I'm not sure I get the political implications, Mrs Farnsworth.

MRS FARNSWORTH: Oh they're coming up.

GORDON: Then maybe we need to hear more.

MRS FARNSWORTH: Trouble is, here's where I've hit sort of a snag.

GORDON: After the first paragraph? Why?

MRS FARNSWORTH: I don't know. Which is why I'm taking your course.

GORDON: So let's roll up our sleeves and get to work.

MRS FARNSWORTH: Now? What about the girl with the cat?

GORDON: *(Indicating the board)* Amy Needleman? I'm sure she'll allow you a few more minutes, won't you, Amy?

AMY: *(From audience)* Oh sure.

MRS FARNSWORTH: Thank you, Miss Needleman.

AMY: Call me Amy.

MRS FARNSWORTH: I'll try.

GORDON: We'll start by talking about your own response to what you just read.

MRS FARNSWORTH: My response?

GORDON: There's a big difference between what goes on in our heads when we are scribbling away at home, and what goes on when we finally make it a public utterance.

MRS FARNSWORTH: Oh boy. Is that true enough!

GORDON: So tell us: how did it feel?

MRS FARNSWORTH: Gosh. *(Pause)* Feel. *(To audience)* Hmmm. *(To* GORDON*)* This is slightly embarrassing.

GORDON: Why?

MRS FARNSWORTH: I hate patting myself on the back.

GORDON: I take it you liked it.

MRS FARNSWORTH: I did. It felt quite nice.

GORDON: Quite nice.

MRS FARNSWORTH: Does that sound like I'm blowing my own horn?

GORDON: Not at all, Mrs Farnsworth. Because it *was* quite nice. It was nicely written, with nice details, and a nice sense of rhythm in the prose.

MRS FARNSWORTH: Why thank you.

GORDON: Quite nice it was. But ...

MRS FARNSWORTH: *(To audience)* There's always a but, isn't there?

GORDON: You said you wanted this to be a book

MRS FARNSWORTH: I do.

GORDON: O K, then: if someone told you that a book was quite nice, would you rush to the book store to buy it?

MRS FARNSWORTH: I might if I knew it had something exciting coming up later on.

GORDON: But we don't know that, do we?

MRS FARNSWORTH: Yes, but I know it. I just can't write it down.

GORDON: Then tell it to us.

MRS FARNSWORTH: You mean now?

GORDON: Sure.

MRS FARNSWORTH: Just *talk* it?

GORDON: Why not?

MRS FARNSWORTH: But is it still my turn?

GORDON: *(Glancing at watch)* It's still your turn, Mrs Farnsworth. We'll give you a few more minutes to talk it through.

MRS FARNSWORTH: O K. *(To audience)* I swear I'll be brief.

GORDON: Go. Go.

3  MRS FARNSWORTH: O K. So after I've written that general picture of skiing in New England in the late 1960s I want to zoom in on.... Can you "zoom in on" things in books?

GORDON: You can when you sell it to the movies.

MRS FARNSWORTH: Oh boy. Don't I wish! All right then, I want to zoom in on this young couple standing in a ski-tow line up at Stowe, and they're arguing like mad. She is almost in tears, and he's trying to calm her down. They talk in whispers, because there are people all around them, but you can tell they're in trouble. And when they climb onto the chair-lift, and at last are alone in the world, the girl really lets loose. And you discover that she's pregnant and he's not nuts about the idea.

GORDON: Pregnancy's good. *(He writes "PREGNANCY" on the board)*

MRS FARNSWORTH: Good? Why?

GORDON: At least it's better than just a bunch of rich preppies sliding idly down a hill.

MRS FARNSWORTH: *(To audience)* See? There's that Greenwich thing again.

GORDON: Sorry. What I mean is, we all identify with pregnancy. Most people have sex. As a result of which, many people get pregnant. Whereas most people don't ski because they don't have the money.

MRS FARNSWORTH: Good point. Anyway, during this argument on the chairlift , you find out that the girl goes to Vassar and the boy goes to Yale...

(GORDON *has gone to his desk, taken other papers out of his backpack, and is beginning to thumb through them.*)

Have you got something else to do?

GORDON: No, no. Go on. I can listen while I'm getting organized here.

MRS FARNSWORTH: All right. *(To audience)* And you begin to suspect that the boy has a slight alcohol problem, since he's been stopping to drink beer all afternoon. And you also discover that he's the scion... *(To* GORDON*)* ...do you pronounce the word "sion" or "skion"...

GORDON: *(Vaguely, as he thumbs through documents)* "Sion" I believe.

MRS FARNSWORTH: You realize the boy is the scion of a distinguished Republican family. His grandfather was a United States senator and his father is an important government official who has Presidential aspirations....

GORDON: *(Looking up)* Whose father?

MRS FARNSWORTH: The boy I'm writing about.

GORDON: *(Putting aside his work)* Go on.

MRS FARNSWORTH: And we also learn more about the girl. You find out she's from Boston—Back Bay, actually, and—

GORDON: You say the boy goes to Yale?

MRS FARNSWORTH: As did his father.

GORDON: And his grandfather was a Senator?

MRS FARNSWORTH: Yes. And—

GORDON: Hold it! *(Goes to the blackboard, writes in big letters: "BUSH !!!????")* Am I right?

MRS FARNSWORTH: About what?

GORDON: You're writing about Bush.

MRS FARNSWORTH: I never use that name.

GORDON: But it's Bush, isn't it?

MRS FARNSWORTH: I never say.

GORDON: Tell me this: is this a personal account?

MRS FARNSWORTH: No. I made some of the stuff up.

GORDON: Did you yourself go to Vassar?

MRS FARNSWORTH: Actually I did.

GORDON: *(To audience)* We're getting warmer.

MRS FARNSWORTH: But the girl in my book is not me. For example, in the book she is taking a creative writing course. Which I never did. Though I'll bet you wish I had.

GORDON: Mrs Farnsworth, let's put it this way. When you were at Vassar, did you happen to know a guy named George W Bush?

MRS FARNSWORTH: Won't tell.

GORDON: Oh come on. The Greenwich connection. The Yale thing. His family's political history. You are writing a book about a woman who gets pregnant by George W Bush!

MRS FARNSWORTH: I'll tell you what I am NOT writing. I am not writing one of those stupid memoirs. *(She erases "BUSH!!!????" from the board)*

GORDON: Nothing wrong with memoirs, Mrs Farnsworth.

MRS FARNSWORTH: Maybe not, but that's not what I want to do. I want to write a good book with a strong political point which people will rush to read.

GORDON: They'll rush to read yours if it's about Bush!

MRS FARNSWORTH: I don't want it to be just that.

GORDON: Nothing wrong with commercial success.

MRS FARNSWORTH: Yes there is, if that's all there is.

GORDON: So what are you going for, then?

MRS FARNSWORTH: That's the problem. I'm not sure. I want to make a dent in things, I really do, but I don't want to make it a cheap shot.

4  GORDON: Mrs Farnsworth: how about defying your grandmother and sitting down?

MRS FARNSWORTH: As a matter of fact I will, because I've got the feeling I'm about to get the third degree. *(She sits.)*

GORDON: Good.

MRS FARNSWORTH: Promise you won't ask what's true and what isn't? That throws me off every time.

GORDON: I promise.

MRS FARNSWORTH: Then shoot.

GORDON: We left your young couple arguing about her pregnancy on the chairlift on the way up a mountain.

MRS FARNSWORTH: I'll tell you how they ski down.

GORDON: Oh come on.

MRS FARNSWORTH: No really. You can learn a lot about people from how they ski. For example—

GORDON: For example, he's probably a lousy skier.

MRS FARNSWORTH: Why?

GORDON: Because he grew up in Texas.

MRS FARNSWORTH: Wrong! I won't say that!

GORDON: You won't mention Texas?

MRS FARNSWORTH: I plan to purposely avoid it. I'll simply say he went to a fancy New England prep school and learned how to ski there.

GORDON: *(Thinking it over)* Right. So go on.

MRS FARNSWORTH: So when they get to the bottom of the mountain, it's pretty much the end of the day, so he drives back to Yale with his friends, and she drives back to Vassar with hers.

GORDON: And?

MRS FARNSWORTH: And they haven't solved their problem. Because she wants him to marry her.

GORDON: Because she's pregnant.

MRS FARNSWORTH: Because she loves him. Or thinks she does. Despite his drinking and hacking around, she's really quite nuts about him. *(To audience)* He's cute as a button, actually, even if he doesn't have much going on upstairs.

GORDON: You say that in your book? That he's not too bright?

MRS FARNSWORTH: Of course not. That would be mean. But I'm hoping people will sense it, just from the way he talks.

GORDON: Right. Go on.

MRS FARNSWORTH: So after they're back at their respective colleges, she tries to telephone him. She leaves messages all over the place, and even sends him a special delivery letter, but there's no answer at all.

GORDON: So we discover his true colors.

MRS FARNSWORTH: Not at all. It's much more complicated than that. She finds out that he can't answer, even if he wanted to.

GORDON: Can't?

MRS FARNSWORTH: Because of the accident.

GORDON: What accident?

MRS FARNSWORTH: On the way back from skiing, they hit someone with their car.

GORDON: What?

MRS FARNSWORTH: He was so upset about her being pregnant that they stopped for more beer. So it was quite late at night when they hit an old man walking down the middle of the road.

GORDON: Did they kill him?

MRS FARNSWORTH: Actually they did.

GORDON: Oh my God!

MRS FARNSWORTH: And they didn't report it.

GORDON: You mean it's a hit and run?

MRS FARNSWORTH: No. Because they claim they weren't aware what they had done. Until they read about it the next morning in the New Haven Register. And then they turned themselves in.

GORDON: Was Bush driving?

MRS FARNSWORTH: Was who driving?

GORDON: Your young man.

MRS FARNSWORTH: Miles. I call him Miles.

GORDON: Was Miles driving?

MRS FARNSWORTH: I keep that purposely vague. One of the boys testifies that Miles was at the wheel, but Miles testifies that he was asleep in the back of the car.

GORDON: So who takes the rap?

MRS FARNSWORTH: Miles's room-mate.

GORDON: He gets his room-mate to take the rap?

MRS FARNSWORTH: I never actually say that. I just have the room-mate say he was driving, so he gets a suspended sentence because the victim was kind of crazy anyway—jay-walking at night down the middle of the road. And later on in the book, I have the room-mate get a very nice job with an oil company in Texas after he graduates from Yale.

GORDON: So you do mention Texas.

MRS FARNSWORTH: My mistake. I'll change it to Oklahoma.

GORDON: No don't! Take us back to...what's his name?

MRS FARNSWORTH: Miles? Well,, with all those hearings and lawyers and depositions and insurance claims and stuff, he hasn't had time to answer his girl-friend's frantic telephone calls from Vassar.

GORDON: But you keep calling him.

MRS FARNSWORTH: Emily...*Emily* keeps calling him. And finally he picks up the phone. So they have this long conversation. She wants to keep the baby and get married. She thinks she can get him to give up drinking once he's away from that wild, partying crowd at Yale. But he won't even admit that the baby's his, the rat.

GORDON: And is it?

MRS FARNSWORTH: Of course it is! What do you take her for? Jesus! *(To audience)* Pardon my French.

GORDON: Sorry, sorry, sorry.

MRS FARNSWORTH: Anyway Miles accuses Emily of having other lovers, which is a big fat lie and he knows it but still says it, which hurts her very much. He also says they're too young to get married, which maybe they are, or at least he is, because he's quite immature. But still they were both over twenty-one, for God's sake, and in those days people got married when they were younger.

GORDON: True enough.

MRS FARNSWORTH: So then he tells her that his family doesn't want him to get married because they feel he has some serious growing up to do, which is true, actually.

GORDON: Still is, actually.

MRS FARNSWORTH: But Emily could damn well help him do it!

GORDON: So she still loves him.

MRS FARNSWORTH: I guess she does. But they split up, and she decides to have the baby just the same.

GORDON: That's very brave.

MRS FARNSWORTH: It isn't as brave as it sounds. She was pretty much fed up with Vassar anyway, with all

the girls majoring in Art Appreciation, and getting the
curse at the same time, and squealing about who got
pinned last weekend at some raucous fraternity party.
So she decides to start a new life out in San Francisco,
bringing up the baby on her own.

GORDON: Sounds gutsy to me.

MRS FARNSWORTH: Maybe. Or maybe just dumb. She
also plans to write a book.

GORDON: Emily wants to write a book?

MRS FARNSWORTH: She's always wanted to write a
book. Even when she was a little girl, she had this
dream of writing a book.

GORDON: So does she write one?

MRS FARNSWORTH: She does not. Because while she's
thinking about doing all this stuff, there's a knock on
the door of her room at Vassar, and this well-dressed
man walks right in, even though it's after hours. How
he got past the Housemother is beyond me. He says
he's a lawyer, and he looks like one in this spiffy gray
suit, and he very politely asks the roommate to get the
hell out so he can talk privately to Emily. Then he gives
Emily a check for ten thousand dollars, and a round
trip ticket to British Honduras, and the name and
address of a doctor there, and asks her to sign a paper
releasing Miles and his family of any responsibility
et cetera et cetera. And she says thanks but no thanks,
but he leaves said documents on her bureau. So she
sits there, and thinks how much she will hurt her own
stuffy family in Boston if she has a baby out of wedlock,
and how they no longer have much money to help her
along, so she...so she.... (*Pause. This is getting tough for
her.*) Well she quits Vassar, and goes to Honduras, and
it's not much fun, frankly. But she comes home and
uses the money that was left from the ten thousand
dollars to help pay the rent in New York while she

looks for a job. *(Pause)* Ten thousand, back then, was a lot of money.

*(Pause)*

GORDON: What happens to Miles?

MRS FARNSWORTH: Oh well, he goes on with his life. She hears about his various ups and downs.

GORDON: Downs?

MRS FARNSWORTH: Drugs. Alcohol. That stuff. And his family keeps bailing him out.

GORDON: I'm sure.

MRS FARNSWORTH: But finally he seems to get his act together—with a little help from his friends, I might add—and ends up being a big wheel.

GORDON: Doing what?

MRS FARNSWORTH: I don't say.

GORDON: You don't say?

MRS FARNSWORTH: Don't you care what happens to Emily?

GORDON: Go ahead.

MRS FARNSWORTH: Well sir, she becomes an excellent travel agent in New York City. Because she knows and loves Europe. So she wins a prize among travel agents. And she does get married...three times, actually... though you have the sense that she never really finds the right man.

GORDON: Any children?

MRS FARNSWORTH: Two. A boy and a girl. With her second husband. Adopted, actually. Because she couldn't have any of her own.

GORDON: Because of Honduras?

MRS FARNSWORTH: I leave that up in the air. But they are wonderful children, both of them. And she's a good mother, or tries to be. But that marriage doesn't last either, so she marries someone else, and ends up living a big, fat, comfortable life in Connecticut.

GORDON: In New Canaan.

MRS FARNSWORTH: No. And not Greenwich, either, thank God! She lives in Darien. Which is a completely different exit on the Merritt Parkway.

GORDON: So you end your book at about where you are now?

MRS FARNSWORTH: I do. With Miles in some important position, and Emily trying to write a book about their past relationship.

*(Pause)*

GORDON: Wow.

MRS FARNSWORTH: What does that mean? "Wow."

GORDON: It means I'm...impressed.

MRS FARNSWORTH: Thank you very much.

GORDON: I'm impressed and I'll tell you why, Mrs Farnsworth. It suggests in no uncertain terms that our current administration is built on hypocrisy, bribery and corruption.

MRS FARNSWORTH: I guess it does.

GORDON: It suggests that underneath a government which is stridently "pro-life", and obsessed with strict, punitive justice, there lies abortion, murder, and serious tampering with the law.

MRS FARNSWORTH: That's it.

GORDON: And that's why I said Wow.

MRS FARNSWORTH: But do you like the people? Do you like the story?

GORDON: I'll tell you this: it's a story that cries to get out before the election.

MRS FARNSWORTH: Fat chance, if I can't get beyond that first paragraph.

GORDON: Maybe you can, if we work together.

MRS FARNSWORTH: Together?

GORDON: I'll help you. Mrs Farnsworth. All the way to the finish line.

MRS FARNSWORTH: Would you?

GORDON: I'll pull this story out of you, by hook or by crook. *(To audience)* Because these things have got to be made public!

MRS FARNSWORTH: I guess I agree.

GORDON: So we'll start immediately, building from the bottom up. You must be working from an outline or a first draft.

MRS FARNSWORTH: Oh sure. I'm not a total airhead.

GORDON: Bring it in to my office tomorrow.

MRS FARNSWORTH: There's a problem with that.

GORDON: What do you mean?

MRS FARNSWORTH: I don't have it any more.

GORDON: You don't have your first draft?

MRS FARNSWORTH: It was destroyed.

GORDON: Destroyed? How?

MRS FARNSWORTH: Do we really have to get into all this? Here? In public? *(Calling out)* Amy Needleman, you must be must be champing at the bit.

AMY: I'm not. I'm really not.

GORDON: Mrs Farnsworth, what happened to your first draft?

MRS FARNSWORTH: My husband destroyed it.

GORDON: Your husband?

MRS FARNSWORTH: At first I thought it was because of the sex scenes. *(To audience)* Because I had sketched in a couple of really juicy ones along the way. *(To GORDON)* But it turns out those weren't the problem at all. It was the political stuff that got to him.

GORDON: Is he a Republican?

MRS FARNSWORTH: Oh yes. He gives huge wads of money to the Republican Party.

GORDON: And then comes home and destroys his wife's book!

MRS FARNSWORTH: I know it. The stinker.

GORDON: How did he do it?

MRS FARNSWORTH: One afternoon last summer, when I was shopping in the city with a couple of friends, he threw it into the fire.

GORDON: Your entire first draft?

MRS FARNSWORTH: Except for my first paragraph.

GORDON: Didn't you have a copy?

MRS FARNSWORTH: No, because it was all hand-written. *(To audience)* My children think I'm hopelessly retro. I can't even manage a typewriter.

GORDON: I am—appalled.

MRS FARNSWORTH: Actually, before he burned it, he took it into his office and had his secretary run it through the Xerox machine.

GORDON: Why?

MRS FARNSWORTH: So he could show it to his lawyer. And you know what the lawyer told him? He said that what I was writing could bring on a major lawsuit.

GORDON: Did that bother you?

MRS FARNSWORTH: It bothered my husband, I'll say that.

GORDON: I suppose the lawyer was a Republican.

MRS FARNSWORTH: Of course. He goes to Washington every other minute.

GORDON: I'll bet he also told your husband that if you ever wrote this book, it could seriously affect the upcoming election.

MRS FARNSWORTH: I wasn't party to that discussion.

GORDON: Mrs Farnsworth, you've got a tiger by the tail here.

MRS FARNSWORTH: I know I do.

GORDON: Which is why your husband burned it!

MRS FARNSWORTH: The good news is that he told me about it. When I got back from New York, he immediately confessed what he had done. He at least had the courtesy to do that.

GORDON: You must have been furious.

MRS FARNSWORTH: I was! I ran around the house slamming doors and screaming like a fish-wife. *(To audience)* You should have seen our dogs. They hid under the piano. *(To* GORDON*)* Thank God the cleaning woman had left for the day.

GORDON: What about that other copy?

MRS FARNSWORTH: I called up the lawyer, and said I wanted it back immediately.

GORDON: What did he say?

MRS FARNSWORTH: He said he was terribly sorry, but his secretary had shredded it by mistake.

GORDON: What? This is outrageous!

MRS FARNSWORTH: The lawyer said I was lucky.

GORDON: Lucky?

MRS FARNSWORTH: Because he had saved me endless heart-ache and pain. As well as substantial legal bills.

GORDON: He also saved the Republican Party from total disaster.

MRS FARNSWORTH: All I know is that it's hard to go back and write something all over again. Your mind has moved on to another place.

GORDON: I know, I know.

MRS FARNSWORTH: My children say this just proves I should learn how to use the computer, because then I'd still have a copy on my "hard drive"—whatever that means.

GORDON: Your husband could have erased that, too.

MRS FARNSWORTH: He does feel very strongly about the whole thing.

GORDON: Jesus. So all you have is...

MRS FARNSWORTH: All I have is this dinky little first paragraph, with everything else just rolling around in my head.

GORDON: Mrs Farnsworth, I'm going to get very personal here.

MRS FARNSWORTH: Uh-oh.

GORDON: No, seriously, have to. I must ask you whether you're still with your husband.

MRS FARNSWORTH: Oh sure.

GORDON: Even after he burned your manuscript?

MRS FARNSWORTH: He didn't want me to get hurt.

GORDON: Bullshit

MRS FARNSWORTH: He says the best thing he could do for me was to nip the whole thing in the bud.

GORDON: That is a complete load of bullshit, Mrs Farnsworth..

MRS FARNSWORTH: Oh no it isn't. He's very concerned. And you know why?

GORDON: Sure. He's a Republican.

MRS FARNSWORTH: No, that's not it. It's because he loves me. *(To audience)* He does. He tells me how much he loves me all the time. Sometimes he sits down at the piano and plays that Cole Porter song where it suddenly goes... *(Singing)* "Do you love me as I love you?"

GORDON: And do you?

MRS FARNSWORTH: Not when he messes around with my personal property, I can tell you that.

GORDON: Mrs Farnsworth, I think you should blow him off.

MRS FARNSWORTH: Oh please.

GORDON: If you want to be a writer, you've got to can the guy. You'll never write another word with a guy like that around.

MRS FARNSWORTH: Could we possibly continue this discussion during your office hours?

GORDON: No, because it applies to all of us... *(To audience; arm around* MRS FARNSWORTH*)* Because if you want to be a serious writer, gang, you've got to make some basic existential choices here. Take me, for example. O K, I've got my Ph.D in American History, so I suppose I could have committed myself to college teaching. Tenure. Security. The whole cop-out. But I didn't do that. I chose to teach part-time. At night For an insulting salary. With no fringe benefits. Lousy office space. Limited use of the library. Fees if I use the gym. No chance of—

MRS FARNSWORTH: I'm not sure what your point is.

GORDON: I'm doing this so I can have more time to write.

MRS FARNSWORTH: Like that poem for *The Nation*.

GORDON: I'm writing more than that, Mrs Farnsworth. I am writing... *(To class)* ...I am in the process of writing a major work about the Jewish experience in these United States. I start with the arrival of my grandfather and move on from there. I have been writing this for six and a half years.

MRS FARNSWORTH: Heavens! What's taking so long?

GORDON: I haven't reached closure.

MRS FARNSWORTH: Closure? What's that?

GORDON: The sense of an ending. I only know I'm not there yet. I do know this, though. You're lucky to have written even one page living with a guy like your husband.

MRS FARNSWORTH: I'd last about a week on my own.

GORDON: Oh come on.

MRS FARNSWORTH: He takes care of me.

GORDON: Is that a good thing?

MRS FARNSWORTH: It is for me.

GORDON: I suppose he's loaded.

MRS FARNSWORTH: Actually he is. And he gives me a very good life.

GORDON: In boring New Canaan?

MRS FARNSWORTH: In the summer we go to Fisher's Island.

GORDON: Where?

MRS FARNSWORTH: It's a kind of final fortress for Wasps. The Jews had Masada, we have Fisher's Island. We sail and play tennis. And play charades at parties. There are a lot of people in the world who'd like a life like that. That's what they hope to get when they move to Greenwich. But of course they don't. And they can't get near Fisher's Island.

GORDON: Does your husband know you're here tonight?

MRS FARNSWORTH: Heavens no. He thinks I'm seeing *Hairspray* with a friend from boarding school.

GORDON: I don't think you should go home.

MRS FARNSWORTH: Oh please.

GORDON: I think you should stay in town. You're welcome to stay with me.

MRS FARNSWORTH: Oh now.

GORDON: I am serious, Mrs Farnsworth. O K, my girl-friend lives there, too. But she'll understand immediately.

MRS FARNSWORTH: *(To audience)* What he's saying is we'll have a chaperone.

GORDON: *(To audience)* What I'm saying is we've got to move fast. *(To* MRS FARNSWORTH*)* We'll give you the bedroom, Mrs Farnsworth, and Alice and I will sleep on the pull-out couch. Tomorrow morning you and I will get right to work.

MRS FARNSWORTH: What do I tell my husband?

GORDON: Say you're visiting a friend.

MRS FARNSWORTH: I don't like to lie.

GORDON: It's no lie at all. I am your friend, more than you know, and I'll try to become a better one.

MRS FARNSWORTH: *(To audience)* I must say this is sort of exciting.

GORDON: It's more than exciting, Mrs Farnsworth. It's essential. This could make a major difference in our country.

MRS FARNSWORTH: Wouldn't that be wonderful! Except...

GORDON: Except what?

MRS FARNSWORTH: Except that I don't want to crank out some stupid political tract which dies right after the election. I want to write something which lasts.

GORDON: You can write something which is both.

*(A loud banging from the back)*

GORDON: If you'll make a major commitment to—

*(Another loud banging)*

GORDON: What the hell is that?

RICK: *(A student sitting far in back)* There's a security guard at the door.

GORDON: Security guard? .

RICK: He wants to speak to you.

GORDON: Why?

RICK: He didn't say.

GORDON: Hmmm. *(To MRS FARNSWORTH)* Don't move. I'll talk to him in the hall. *(He starts off.)*

MRS FARNSWORTH: *(Calling after him)* What am I supposed to do? Just *stand* here?

GORDON: *(Over his shoulder)* This won't take a minute. *(He hurries off.)*

*(Pause)*

MRS FARNSWORTH: *(Nervously, to audience)* I have no idea what I'm supposed to do.

AMY: *(From audience)* Tell us more about your book.

RICK: *(From the back)* Tell us how it ends.

MRS FARNSWORTH: I've already told you. It ends with Emily trying to write this book.

JANET: *(Another student in the audience; she might be sitting in the first row far over to one side.)* That's not much of an ending.

MRS FARNSWORTH: I know it. Maybe I'll put in one last chapter. Where Miles and Emily meet one more time, later on, when they're older. He's now king of the hill, so to speak, and she's a suburban lady of a certain age. And there's a big fund-raiser, which her husband has paid ten thousand dollars to go to. And the fund-raiser is for guess who. So she goes, and stands in line to meet him, because she's secretly hoping she can take him aside and tell him to grow up, for God's sake. But when she finally gets to shake his hand, you know what he says? He says, "Hi there". Can you believe it? Just "Hi there." Anyone who says that ought to be shot. It means they don't know your name and are pretending they do. It's the "there" that gets me. It's kind of putting you in your place. Now it's been a long time since they've seen each other, and her hair is different, but still he doesn't even remember. Or worse: maybe he does, and won't admit it. In any case, this experience makes her so mad that she goes home and sits down to write that book she's always wanted to write. So my book ends with Emily starting to write hers. Only now you think maybe she'll be able to do it. *(Pause)* Is that sort of confusing?

RICK: Sounds cool...

MRS FARNSWORTH: Or corny? Is it too corny? It might be a little corny.

AMY: May I ask a question?

MRS FARNSWORTH: Absolutely.

AMY: Does she write this book out of anger?

MRS FARNSWORTH: Yes. I guess she does. Anger, because he doesn't even remember. And anger, because he's doing such a terrible job.

AMY: I don't know. Anger. I don't think that's a good place to write from.

RICK: It's a good place to start from.

JANET: I think she's angry because she still loves him.

MRS FARNSWORTH: What?

JANET: I'm saying maybe she still loves him.

MRS FARNSWORTH: Now that's just about the silliest thing I ever heard in my entire life.

*(GORDON comes back in.)*

GORDON: Mrs Farnsworth... *(Hurrying down the aisle)* I need to speak to you a minute.

MRS FARNSWORTH: Me?

GORDON: There's a problem.

*(He takes her to a corner upstage, starts whispering to her.)*

MRS FARNSWORTH: *(As he is whispering)* What?...

*(He whispers.)*

MRS FARNSWORTH: Where?...

*(He whispers.)*

MRS FARNSWORTH: Now?...

*(He whispers.)*

MRS FARNSWORTH: Did you say we were in the middle of a class?

GORDON: *(To audience)* Excuse us. This is a private matter. *(More whispering)*

MRS FARNSWORTH: *(Breaking out of it)* You know what? This is rude, what we're doing. Whispering in public.

GORDON: I just thought....

MRS FARNSWORTH: I'm sorry. These people paid good money for this course. They have a right to know what's going on. *(To audience)* He's saying my husband is here.

GORDON: *(To audience)* Waiting, down by the front desk.

MRS FARNSWORTH: *(To audience)* He wants to speak to me. *(To GORDON)* Why didn't he just come up?

GORDON: According to the security guard, he didn't want to disturb the class.

MRS FARNSWORTH: Typical! So now I'm supposed to drop everything and dash downstairs at his beck and call!

GORDON: Don't do it.

MRS FARNSWORTH: I certainly won't.

GORDON: How did he know you were here? I thought you told him you were at the theatre.

MRS FARNSWORTH: He probably had me followed.

GORDON: He'd do that?

MRS FARNSWORTH: He's done it before.

GORDON: Oh God! What kind of a man is her?

MRS FARNSWORTH: A very determined man, I'll tell you that.

GORDON: A very dangerous man.

MRS FARNSWORTH: Oh no. Not dangerous.

GORDON: Controlling, then. How about that? He's a controlling man.

MRS FARNSWORTH: Come to think of it, I'd better go down.

GORDON: Why?

MRS FARNSWORTH: Otherwise he'll come up.

GORDON: Let him.

MRS FARNSWORTH: No siree. I don't want that. He can be quite embarrassing.

GORDON: Look, we'll send down a student. To say you're tied up.

RICK: *(From the back)* I'll go!

GORDON: Who are you?

RICK: Rick Costello.

GORDON: Rick Costello will go.

RICK: I'm on my way.

MRS FARNSWORTH: No, don't. Please.

RICK: I want to meet the guy.

MRS FARNSWORTH: No, this is my problem. Please sit back down. *(To GORDON)* He's my husband, after all.

RICK: O K, Mrs Farnsworth.

MRS FARNSWORTH: But before I leave, I've a little job to do. *(She opens her bag, takes out a compact, starts repairing her lipstick.)*

GORDON: Why are you doing that?

MRS FARNSWORTH: Habit, I guess.

GORDON: He makes you wear make-up?

MRS FARNSWORTH: Just the reverse. He hates it. He says it's gilding the lily. I have to sneak it on when he's not around.

AMY: Why bother?

MRS FARNSWORTH: Because he thinks I'm beautiful and I'd hate to disillusion him. *(She combs her hair.)*

JANET: What do you plan to say to him?

MRS FARNSWORTH: I'll say, "Go home, Forrest."

GORDON: Forrest?

MRS FARNSWORTH: It's his mother's maiden name. Lots of Republicans do that to their children. *(Putting her compact back in her purse)*

GORDON: I'll bet you won't come back.

MRS FARNSWORTH: Oh yes I will. In fact, to make you feel better, I'll leave a deposit.... *(She puts her bag pointedly on the desk.)*

GORDON: What if he gets rough?

MRS FARNSWORTH: Listen, you. One thing about my husband. He's a perfect gentleman, at all times.

GORDON: Yeah right. Burning your manuscript, having you followed.

MRS FARNSWORTH: All because he loves me. *(She starts out.)*

GORDON: Some love.

MRS FARNSWORTH: Yes. Well. There's love and there's love.

GORDON: Remember, we've still got a lot of stuff to do here, Mrs Farnsworth.

MRS FARNSWORTH: Yes, we've got to hear about that cat.

GORDON: Fuck the cat!

MRS FARNSWORTH: *(Stopping, turning)* Now that remark was uncalled for.

GORDON: I mean we may have to forego the cat.

MRS FARNSWORTH: *(As she goes)* That sounds much more attractive. *(She's off.)*

*(GORDON sits and thinks.)*

GORDON: *(Finally; to audience)* O K. A question. *(He goes to the blackboard, writes: "HARRIET BEECHER STOWE")* Who was she?

AMY: *(From audience)* Everyone knows that.

RICK: *(From the back)* A recently naturalized citizen might not.

AMY: O K, O K. She wrote *Uncle Tom's Cabin*.

GORDON: And what did Abraham Lincoln say to her when he met her?

RICK: He said "Hi there."

GORDON: Funny guy. Anyone else?

*(JANET raises her hand.)*

Yes. Uh, Janet, isn't it? What did Lincoln say, Janet?

JANET: Didn't he say "Your book started the Civil War"? Something like that?

GORDON: He said it better. He said, "So you're the little lady who started this big war." And why did he say that?

AMY: Because her book showed the world what slavery looked like, up close and personal.

GORDON: So the North was willing to fight to eliminate it.

AMY: What does that have to do with Mrs Farnsworth?

GORDON: Ah hah. That's the question. What does Harriet Beecher Stowe have to do with Mrs Forrest Farnsworth? *(He draws an arrow connecting the two names on the board.)*

AMY: Both women wrote books.

GORDON: Yes. Although one of them is still *trying* to write one.

*(JANET raises her hand.)*

Yes, Janet...

JANET: And both books deal with major political issues.

GORDON: Yes. And...

AMY: Yeah, but Mrs Farnsworth's book won't start any war!

GORDON: No, you're right. But Mrs Farnsworth's book could do something better. Mrs Farnsworth's book could *stop* a war.

JANET: You mean the war in Iraq?

GORDON: No, I don't mean the war in Iraq, though let's hope it could do that, too.. No I'm thinking of the much more subversive war which George W Bush and that clique of Republican retros around him have been fighting ever since the guy was not—repeat, *not* —elected. I'm thinking of their war against a clean and renewable natural environment. I'm thinking of their war against a coherent fiscal policy and an equitable system of taxation. I'm thinking of their war against a fair judicial system, and against our international obligations, and against our basic human responsibilities all over the world. This is the war that Mrs Farnsworth's book could stop by getting those creeps out of office. Because if we can get it written, get it published, get it out there, she will show the world

not the face of slavery, but the face of the blind, selfish,
unwarranted power now presiding in Washington.

RICK: Yes!

GORDON: Thanks, Rick.

(AMY *raises her hand.*)

GORDON: Amy?

AMY: Don't you think she's taking too long a time
down there?

GORDON: *(Checking his watch)* You may be right.

AMY: I mean, how long does it take for a woman to tell
her husband she's in the middle of a class?

JANET: Maybe someone better go down and check.

RICK: I'll go.

GORDON: Hold it! Give her a few more minutes, Rick.
That woman is sitting on a keg of dynamite. Let's not
create any more sparks than we have to.

JANET: Do you think she's in danger?

GORDON: I tell you what I think.... *(Goes to blackboard,
writes "MARTHA MITCHELL.")* Anyone know who
Martha Mitchell was? *(Looks out)* No? Neither did I,
till I recently read a book about Watergate.

RICK: Wait! Martha Mitchell was...um....

GORDON: Martha Mitchell was the wife of the Attorney
General of the United States under Nixon.

RICK: Oh yeah.

GORDON: And she knew stuff.. Stuff she shouldn't
know. Republican stuff. Stuff she wanted to tell the
press. But the F B I got wind of it. Or the C I A. Or both,
most likely, the way things were at that time. So they
came to her apartment, threw her down on the bed,

shot a sedative into her butt , and then shipped her
off to some funny farm where she couldn't blab.
*(Goes to blackboard, draws arrows connecting* MARTHA
MITCHELL *to* MRS FARNSWORTH *and to* HARRIET
BEECHER STOWE*)* And having said that, I now find
myself just a little more worried about our friend Mrs
Farnsworth . Maybe, Rick, it's time for you to....

10   *(A male voice is heard from the back)*

FARNSWORTH: *(Calling out)* Excuse me!

69 ?   GORDON: *(Peering out)* Yes?

FARNSWORTH: May I intrude on your class for one brief
moment? *(He appears in the aisle. He is an attractive,*
more ?   *middle-aged man, in a tailored business suit.)*
preppy

GORDON: And you are...?

FARNSWORTH: Forrest Farnsworth...

GORDON: *(To audience)* The husband.

*(Boos and groans from the students)*

FARNSWORTH: *(To audience)* Yes. The husband. And
proud to be so. And I'm here to retrieve my wife's
purse.

GORDON: She told us about you, sir.

FARNSWORTH: Good things, I hope.

GORDON: Not entirely.

FARNSWORTH: Sorry to hear that. *(Pointing to the purse
on the desk)* Ah hah. I spy! Forgive me, but may I slightly
encroach upon your territory? I'll just reclaim my prize,
if I may, and make a discreet departure.

GORDON: *(Quickly grabbing the purse)* One minute please.

FARNSWORTH: There's some difficulty?

GORDON: Where is your wife?

JANET: Yes. Where is Mrs Farnsworth?

FARNSWORTH: Ah.

GORDON: Yes. Ah.

FARNSWORTH: *(To audience)* I wonder, how many times over the centuries has a husband been asked that very same question? "Where is your wife?" And how many times has he been unable to answer?

AMY: The guy is stalling.

RICK: The guy is bullshit.

GORDON: Are you saying you don't know?

FARNSWORTH: I think I know. I hope I know. But are we ever sure?

RICK: He's a wise guy.

GORDON: I don't get you, sir.

FARNSWORTH: I think it's safe to say that my wife is sitting in the car.

GORDON: Sitting in the car?

FARNSWORTH: While I retrieve her purse. Before I drive her home.

AMY: What car?

FARNSWORTH: *(Patiently)* A dependable pearl-gray 1993 Volvo station wagon, which I have managed to keep alive for well over ten years.

JANET: *(Calling out)* Why is she sitting in the car?

RICK: Yeah. Why?

FARNSWORTH: Because I'm double-parked and don't want it towed away...

GORDON: We mean why isn't she coming back to class?

FARNSWORTH: Ah...

GORDON: *(To audience)* Another ah,

FARNSWORTH: She is not coming back because there has been a slight accident.

GORDON: Accident?

FARNSWORTH: My dear wife has somehow managed to sprain her ankle.

GORDON: Get out of here.

FARNSWORTH: I'm sorry, but that's what she's done. And so now she's waiting in the car so I can drive her home, and put some ice on her ankle, and somewhat reduce the swelling. *(Takes the purse from GORDON, starts out)*

RICK: I don't believe you, mister!

JANET: Neither do I.

AMY: I'm on the fence.

FARNSWORTH: *(To GORDON)* You seem to be teaching a very skeptical group.

STUDENTS: She was just here.... This is so unbelievable.... We weren't born yesterday....

GORDON: *(To students)* Hold it. Calm down. *(To FARNSWORTH)* I don't believe you either.

FARNSWORTH: What don't you believe?

GORDON: The whole story.

FARNSWORTH: Then let's go over it, step by step. Do you believe that my wife was in a hurry to come down and speak to me so that she could quickly return to your class?

GORDON: Yes . I believe that. *(To students)* O K? We can believe that?

STUDENTS: Sure... Maybe... I dunno....

FARNSWORTH: And do you believe that she took the staircase next to the elevator, because it would provide some physical exercise?

GORDON: O K, yes.

RICK: Possibly.

JANET: She said she didn't like elevators.

FARNSWORTH: All right then. And do you believe that a student, or students, might have spilled a gooey gob of something called a pineapple smoothie on the bottom few stairs?

*? looked like apparent to be.*

GORDON: Maybe. Yes.

JANET: Actually that might have been me.

FARNSWORTH: You spilled that smoothie?

JANET: On the way to class.

FARNSWORTH: And didn't clean it up, apparently.

JANET: *(Grumpily)* I'm sorry.

FARNSWORTH: Then you should be the first one to believe that my dear wife rushed down the stairs, slipped on your spilled smoothie, and twisted her ankle before she fell into my arms.

*? she*

JANET: *(Irritably)* O K. Whatever.

FARNSWORTH: Then I'll be on my way. *(Holding out his hand)* Goodbye, sir.

GORDON: *(Not taking his hand)* Your wife told us some heavy stuff about you, Mr Farnsworth.

FARNSWORTH: (Still holding out his hand) Did she tell you not to shake hands?

*my*

GORDON: No. *(Reluctantly shaking hands)* I'm Gordon Bell.

FARNSWORTH: Delighted to meet you, Professor.

GORDON: I'm no professor. I am lowly part-time
lecturer.

FARNSWORTH: (Patting him on the back) Cheer up,
my man. Titles can be totally misleading. (To audience)
I know a Chairman of the Board who knows less about
his company than his assistant foreman. (To GORDON,
indicating the audience) And this, I assume, is your class
in creative writing. (He surveys them.) They seem like
a no-nonsense group! It must be challenging to bring
them into line. (To class) Pay attention to your teacher,
my friends. Work hard. Write clear, complete sentences.
Keep an eye on your punctuation. (He starts out again.)
And now I'm off.

GORDON: Would you answer a few more questions, sir?

FARNSWORTH: All right. As long as they don't take too
much time. My better half hates to wait. She makes me
do it all the time, of course, but when I do it back, she
becomes restless and irritable.

GORDON: How did you know she'd be here?

FARNSWORTH: Ah.

GORDON: Did you have her followed?

FARNSWORTH: Have her followed? Good heavens, no.
I followed her myself.

GORDON: On the train?

FARNSWORTH: No. She took the train. I drove in by car.

GORDON: Didn't she tell you she was going to *Hairspray*?

FARNSWORTH: She did indeed. But I didn't believe her.

GORDON: You don't trust your own wife?

FARNSWORTH: I don't trust *Hairspray*. She's seen it
before, and I suspected once was enough.

GORDON: Then how...?

FARNSWORTH: *(Patiently)* She left the course catalogue open on the kitchen table, having carefully circled this class, including where and when it met. Now may I leave?

GORDON: Do you do this a lot, Mr Farnsworth?

FARNSWORTH: Ask to leave?

GORDON: Intrude on your wife's activities.

FARNSWORTH: Probably too much.

GORDON: I think so.

FARNSWORTH: Now how do I explain this? My wife is like a lovely rainbow trout. In order to keep her in play, I like to maintain a taut line.

GORDON: So the hook stays in her mouth?

FARNSWORTH: So she won't get away.

GORDON: Do you think she'd like hearing you saying that?

FARNSWORTH: I think she'd hate it. Which makes me glad she's waiting in the car. *(Starts off again)*

GORDON: Why don't you want her to take this course?

FARNSWORTH: Ah.

GORDON: *(To audience)* Always these ah's.

FARNSWORTH: *(To audience)* I don't want her to take this course because she could ruin the class.

GORDON: She hasn't ruined it yet.

FARNSWORTH: Good. Then I showed up in time.

GORDON: What makes you think she'd ruin the class?

FARNSWORTH: Because... *(Noticing the blackboard with its various markings)* This looks like an extremely interesting course.

GORDON: It is indeed.

FARNSWORTH: Harriet Beecher Stowe...Martha Mitchell? I assume you mean *Margaret* Mitchell ~~who wrote~~ *Gone With the Wind.*

*for* ?

GORDON: I mean Martha. And I still want to know why your wife will ruin us.

FARNSWORTH: Politics.

GORDON: Politics?

FARNSWORTH: My wife has a tendency to gravitate towards political subjects.

GORDON: *(Dryly)* Oh really?

? FARNSWORTH: Subjects which don't belong in a writing class.

GORDON: Why do you think that?

FARNSWORTH: Because political writing and political discussions ~~are~~ simple-minded and reductive. They always boil down to a frantic exchange of information, most of it wrong. In the end, they cause nothing but argument and controversy. *(To class)* As opposed to good writing. Which should be subtle, ~~complicated~~ and ambiguous.

*tend to be*

*complex?*

GORDON: I see.

FARNSWORTH: To add to the difficulty, my wife is also—though it pains me to say it—somewhat leftist in her leanings.

GORDON: *(To audience)* Surprise, surprise.

FARNSWORTH: And frankly—this is no place to get into this, I know—but she is totally obsessed by one subject.

GORDON: And what is that?

FARNSWORTH: She is obsessed by what she feels are the crimes and misdemeanors of our current administration.

GORDON: Oh really?

FARNSWORTH: Particularly our chief executive. Push that button and she's off to the races. She has managed to decimate several Connecticut dinner parties on that very subject. And last week she was banished from her tennis group for bringing up Bush in the ladies' locker room.

GORDON: *(To audience)* Well, well.

FARNSWORTH: In fact—oh Lord, I don't know whether to bring this up or not—but lately, she has been trying to write an entire book about him...

GORDON: Mr Farnsworth.

FARNSWORTH: Yes?

GORDON: We're way ahead of you here.

FARNSWORTH: Ahead of me?

GORDON: Your wife has already mentioned her book.

FARNSWORTH: Already? Why the term has hardly begun!

GORDON: She specifically asked to go to the head of the line. She has even read us her first paragraph.

FARNSWORTH: I like that paragraph actually, I'm very fond of it. *(To audience)* I hope you liked it. And I hope you told her so.

GORDON: We all liked it, sir. And we all also liked the rest of her plot.

FARNSWORTH: She told you the plot?

GORDON: A few minutes ago.

FARNSWORTH: Then I'm too late after all!

GORDON: Yes, you are, Mr Farnsworth. Because everyone in this room now knows the whole, sad story .

FARNSWORTH: All I can do then is apologize.

GORDON: What she told us needs no apology, thanks.

FARNSWORTH: I believe it does. Because it isn't true.

GORDON: What?

FARNSWORTH: It's a piece of fiction, top to bottom....

GORDON: It's disguised as fiction. That we realize.

FARNSWORTH: But it can easily be perceived as being true.

GORDON: Damn right.

FARNSWORTH: And cause serious harm to ~~other~~ people.

GORDON: Such as to Bush?

FARNSWORTH: Such as to many people.

GORDON: Is that why you destroyed her first draft?

FARNSWORTH: Destroyed her what?

GORDON: The first draft of her book.

FARNSWORTH: Is that what's she's calling it now? A "first draft"? (*Laughing*) Those scribblings on scrap paper and the backs of old Christmas cards?

GORDON: Whatever it was, you shouldn't have burned it.

FARNSWORTH: She told you I *burned* it?

GORDON: In your fireplace last summer.

FARNSWORTH: (*Laughing*) I must say she has a glorious imagination. (*To audience*) Do I look like the kind of a man who would start a good wood fire on Fisher's Island in the middle of August?

GORDON: What kind of a man are you, Mr Farnsworth?

FARNSWORTH: I'm an orderly man. Not fastidious, but orderly. I like things to be somewhat ship-shape, at least in my own home. And so I'll admit that last summer, in a futile attempt to restore a modicum of tidiness to our living room, I may have inadvertently thrown out some of my wife's, well, "stuff", as she calls it. She strews so much around—shopping lists, J Crew catalogues, clippings from *The Nation* and *The New York Review of Books*—and so, when I was doing a little re-organizing, I may have taken her so-called "first draft"— *(Laughing again)* ...did she really call it that? —and delivered it to the town dump.

GORDON: She said you burned it.

FARNSWORTH: Because she's an artist, God love her! She adjusts, she amplifies, she exaggerates! Which is why I don't want her here. It's obviously more exciting to say her manuscript was burned than to say some scrap paper disappeared into a dumpster.

GORDON: You're a clever guy, Mr Farnsworth.

FARNSWORTH *(Bowing)* Thank you, sir.

GORDON: But again I have to say I don't believe you. Seeing as how you slipped a copy of her draft to your lawyer

*(Pause)*

FARNSWORTH: Oh that.

GORDON: Yes that.

FARNSWORTH: I must say she's a consistent storyteller.... All right. Yes. Earlier in the summer I showed my lawyer a few sheets of what she was writing which he glanced at, and shredded immediately.

GORDON: Some of us here would very much like to know why.

FARNSWORTH: Because he felt that certain plot points in her story could be interpreted as applying to himself.

*mis?*

GORDON: Applying to your *lawyer*?

FARNSWORTH: Yes, apparently there was a page or two which seemed to accuse him of arranging an abortion on behalf of—never mind. It was an outrageous accusation and potentially libelous, so he very wisely destroyed it. *(To audience)* As for you good people, I'm sorry you had to sit through her whole sad, sordid fabrication.

GORDON: How do we know it isn't all basically true?

*II*

FARNSWORTH: Because... *(Pause)* Because... *(Pause; to audience)* I am now going to have to call on the discretion of everyone in this room. I'm serious now. I don't want to hear of any of this showing up on one *of* your stupid chat-rooms on the internet. I am going to assume that everyone here has a certain decent respect for the privacy of others. Or is that too much to assume?

GORDON: You can count on me, and I hope that you can count on everyone else.

*with just*

FARNSWORTH: Which means, I suppose, that, as in most things in life , we have to hold our noses and go on faith.

GORDON: We're waiting, sir.

FARNSWORTH: *(After a pause)* My wife is not well.

GORDON: I'm not sure what you mean.

FARNSWORTH: She's been hospitalized twice. Once, a few years ago, for a bout of alcoholism, from which, thank God, she seems to have recovered.

GORDON: No kidding.

*?*

FARNSWORTH: And then again, later on, for a kind of general depression.

*more recently*

GORDON: I didn't know that.

FARNSWORTH: Well, now you do. The word for it these days, they tell me, is bi-polar. She can be up, she can be down. *(To audience)* Tonight you seem to have caught her at the top of her bounce.

GORDON: Oh boy.

FARNSWORTH: *But* There have been times when...when ? she hasn't liked herself very much. *(Pause)* And many more times when she hasn't liked *me*. This woman who means everything in the world to me, whom I adore beyond anything else in my life, she...well I'll give you an example. The other night I looked up from my reading to see her staring at me from across the room, as if I were some alien creature from another planet.

GORDON: Oh well. We all /.

FARNSWORTH: No, No. You don't understand. She looked at me if ... as if she didn't love me any more. ? as *(He turns his back to the audience, takes out his handkerchief.* ? *There is a pause, then he wipes his eyes, turns back to the audience.)* I suppose she told you I was her third husband and she had two adopted children by her second?

GORDON: She sort of said that. Yes.

FARNSWORTH: She's been "sort of" saying it more and more. How do you think I feel when I hear that *kind* sort of ? thing? How do our children feel? My wife and I have been married for thirty-four years and our children are 35 ? very much our natural offspring.

GORDON: I see.

FARNSWORTH: They're out of the nest now, thank God, and immersed in their own lives. As for me...well, it can be very painful, personally, to live with these things.

GORDON: I suppose the families of writers have to suffer a lot.

FARNSWORTH: Yes indeed. It was her therapist's idea, you know. That damn book. ~~She~~ My wife was so upset about how Bush has been behaving that ~~he~~ the therapist suggested she write things down.

GORDON: She knew Bush, didn't she?

FARNSWORTH: Oh well, she may have gone out with him once or twice, back in the middle ages. A couple of her friends from Vassar have said they were briefly an item.

GORDON: So there's a chance that....

FARNSWORTH: I know, I know. Which is why I coughed up a handsome check for that Republican fund-raiser last year when Bush came to town. And dragged her to it. I wanted to see what happened when they actually met. But when she went through the line and shook his hand, I could tell immediately that he didn't even recognize her.

GORDON: Or didn't want to.

FARNSWORTH: Possibly.

GORDON: Probably.

FARNSWORTH: Why probably?

GORDON: In view of the hit and run thing.

FARNSWORTH: Oh good Lord, she even got into that?

GORDON: She got into everything.

FARNSWORTH: Then you should know that I have checked the New Haven court records. There is absolutely nothing there.

GORDON: The records could have been removed.

FARNSWORTH: Highly unlikely.

GORDON: Oh yes? What about his attendance record in the National Guard? What about that car accident in Texas?

FARNSWORTH: What car accident?

GORDON: You see? It's a Watergate world these days, Mr Farnsworth. Records disappear. Or are sealed by the White House.

FARNSWORTH: Or people become paranoid. *(Indicating blackboard)* Like poor Martha Mitchell.

GORDON: Too many of your wife's details have the ring of truth.

FARNSWORTH: What if they do?

GORDON: What if they *do*? You're admitting it now?

FARNSWORTH: It's all water over the dam, my boy. Time to move on. Even her therapist tells her that. But she won't let go.

GORDON: Thank God she won't.

FARNSWORTH: *(Very seriously)* No! No! Think about *her* for a moment. Suppose she finally organizes that stuff into a book. Suppose it gets out. Suppose it hits a true chord here and there. What then? Do you think the Bush people will take it lying down? I know that gang, my friend. I know them very well. They'll counterattack with everything they've got. Do you think for one minute I want my dear wife badgered by the press, joked about on late-night television, and ultimately dismissed as some Connecticut Paula Jones? Do you think I'd enjoy that? Do you think she would?

*(MRS FARNSWORTH's voice is heard from the rear.)*

MRS FARNSWORTH: *(Calling out)* I'd hate it!

FARNSWORTH: *(To GORDON)* Speak of angels, they might appear.

*(To* MRS FARNSWORTH *as she limps on)*

FARNSWORTH: You're supposed to be sitting quietly in the car, dear.

MRS FARNSWORTH: I just paid the Security Guard twenty dollars to do exactly that.

FARNSWORTH: Smart move, darling. But what about your ankle?

MRS FARNSWORTH: I bribed a student to run to the nearest drug store for an ace bandage. Turned out he was a pre-med. See what he did for my leg! *(Her leg is now neatly wrapped.)*

FARNSWORTH: It's a lovely leg, dear. But you shouldn't be walking on it.

MRS FARNSWORTH: I'm perfectly fine. (To audience) Did he tell you how this happened?

FARNSWORTH: I did.

MRS FARNSWORTH: I'll bet he didn't tell you I was pushed.

FARNSWORTH: You slipped on a pineapple smoothie, sweetheart.

MRS FARNSWORTH: I distinctly felt a push from the rear.

FARNSWORTH: *(Getting a chair for her)* Who would possibly want to push you downstairs, dear?

MRS FARNSWORTH: Maybe that lawyer friend of yours.

FARNSWORTH: Oh darling, no.

MRS FARNSWORTH: *(To audience)* I'm sorry. But that's what I think.

FARNSWORTH: *(To audience)* You see? You see what I'm up against? *(To* MRS FARNSWORTH*)* So how long have you been here, dear? Have you heard any of our conversation?

MRS FARNSWORTH: Why? Have you been talking behind my back?

FARNSWORTH: You talked behind mine, darling. You told them I followed you around, burning manuscripts and things.

MRS FARNSWORTH: Oh right. I did, didn't I? O K, fair's fair. *(To audience, lightly)* I'll bet he's been telling you that I'm nuttier than a fruitcake.

FARNSWORTH: I didn't put it that way, dear.

MRS FARNSWORTH: Oh right. You're much too tactful.

FARNSWORTH: *(Taking her to a chair)* At least sit down, please. *(Bringing another chair)* And put your foot up.

MRS FARNSWORTH: *(To audience, as she sits)* He's a very considerate man. But whenever I get even remotely political, he tells people I belong in the loony bin.

FARNSWORTH: I do not, darling!

MRS FARNSWORTH: *(To the audience)* Lord knows I've had my problems in the past. But it doesn't make any difference because I'm on the warpath now.

FARNSWORTH: What does that mean, exactly?

MRS FARNSWORTH: It means I'm ready to name names in my book. *(To GORDON)* And I'll take any help I can get.

GORDON: What changed your mind?

MRS FARNSWORTH: I'll tell you exactly what. While I was sitting twiddling my thumbs in the car, I happened to turn on National Public Radio. And I heard about more of our boys being killed in Iraq. And more Iraqis, too. And how we're in debt up to our elbows. And how everybody hates us, all over the world. And I realized just how much damage George Bush has done in three short years. So I decided to stop fooling around.

GORDON: Bravo!

MRS FARNSWORTH: So I'll take your offer to jump-start me. I'll stay at your place.

GORDON: You're welcome to stay as long as you want.

MRS FARNSWORTH: No, I'll only stay three days, which is already too long , according to my grandmother. Then I'll find a room of my own.

FARNSWORTH: What's happening here?

MRS FARNSWORTH: Quiet, dear. We're making plans. *(To* GORDON*)* Tomorrow morning at the crack of dawn I want you to rush out to Radio Shack and buy a tape recorder. I'll pay the bill

GORDON: I've already got one.

MRS FARNSWORTH: All the better. Then I'll dictate the whole story into your machine. You can type it up as I go along, and point the finger at Bush as much as you want. I'll correct your punctuation and grammar because I learned how to do that at boarding school.

GORDON: My computer will do that for us. And make plenty of copies besides.

FARNSWORTH: I don't like what I'm hearing.

MRS FARNSWORTH: Don't kibitz, Forrest. *(To* GORDON*)* Then we'll send those copies out all over the place.

GORDON: It's called multiple submissions. And within the week, twenty publishers will be bidding their asses off.

MRS FARNSWORTH: Excellent!

*(They give each other the high five.)*

MRS FARNSWORTH: And we'll split the proceeds fifty-fifty. Do you think we need an agent?

FARNSWORTH: Oh good grief.

GORDON: A lawyer, maybe.

MRS FARNSWORTH: *(With a glance at* FARNSWORTH*)* No lawyers, please... *(Indicating audience)* There are plenty of witnesses right here to confirm the deal. *(Getting up, limping downstage to the audience on the arm of* GORDON*)* And if Ashcroft throws us in jail, we'll have plenty of company, because now you're all co-conspirators.

STUDENTS: Oh yeah!... We're with you, baby.... Bring it on!

FARNSWORTH: Darling, please. Hold your horses.

MRS FARNSWORTH: We can't. The election's right around the corner.

FARNSWORTH: So what?

MRS FARNSWORTH: So what? You can't be serious.

FARNSWORTH: Huh. Suppose Bush gets reelected. Is that really the end of the world?

MRS FARNSWORTH: It damn well might be.

FARNSWORTH: No, sweetheart, no. We've lived with inadequate presidents before. Chester Arthur...Millard Fillmore...the country has survived them.

GORDON: That was when we didn't have television to show us first-hand how incompetent they were.

MRS FARNSWORTH: Exactly! And when we weren't a world power and capable of doing such ghastly damage all over the place.

GORDON: There you go, Mrs F!

FARNSWORTH: Mrs F? Isn't that a little fresh? Next thing we know you'll be calling her Margery.

GORDON: I'd sure like to.

FARNSWORTH: Well you can't, unless you've kissed her.

GORDON: I'll make my move while we're working on our book.

FARNSWORTH: See why I hate this book thing, darling? Now it's encouraging you to misbehave with a college professor.

GORDON: Just a lowly lecturer.

FARNSWORTH: All the worse.

MRS FARNSWORTH: It doesn't make any difference who I kiss anyway, because my feelings are totally focused on my book.

FARNSWORTH: (To audience) She's been sitting too long in that car. (To MRS FARNSWORTH) You're high as a kite, sweetheart.

MRS FARNSWORTH: Maybe I am. But who cares?

FARNSWORTH: (Passionately) I care! Very much! So I'm going to be very frank with you, even in front of all these people.

MRS FARNSWORTH: Go ahead. I can take it.

FARNSWORTH: First of all, you'll never write that book.

MRS FARNSWORTH: Says who?

FARNSWORTH: Says me. (To audience) She's incapable of doing it, tape recorder or not. (Indicating GORDON) And no matter who tries to egg her on. (To MRS FARNSWORTH) And even if this man does most of the writing, you'll still end up putting the kibosh on the whole project.

MRS FARNSWORTH: May I possibly know why?

FARNSWORTH: Be prepared. I'm going to say something which will make you and everyone else in this room very, very angry.

MRS FARNSWORTH: Come on. Out with it.

FARNSWORTH: O K. Here goes. You can't do it because every time you try to say something specific about George Bush, ~~you~~ feel like a traitor.

*you'll ?*

MRS FARNSWORTH: A traitor? A traitor to what, for God's sake? My country? Bush is the traitor to everything it stands for.

FARNSWORTH: Maybe, but you'd be a traitor to your class.

MRS FARNSWORTH: My class?

GORDON: I can't believe I'm hearing this.

MRS FARNSWORTH: That is the most ridiculous thing you've ever said!

FARNSWORTH: I knew you'd explode.

MRS FARNSWORTH: What class where? I like to think we've moved beyond that crap!

GORDON: This happens to be a democracy, Farnsworth.

FARNSWORTH: I know it's is a tricky subject, especially in this country. But class exists, or it did once upon a time. And it's still here for Margery Farnsworth. (*To* MRS FARNSWORTH) It was there for you from the day you were born, darling, and it profoundly affects what you think and do. And you know in your deep heart's core that you can't write your book without becoming a traitor to the values you were brought up with.

GORDON: What values I'd like to know.

MRS FARNSWORTH: Yes. Exactly. We don't have any values, except bad ones. Look at our parents. Your father was a drunk, and my mother was a bigot. (*To audience*) And my Uncle James went to jail for tax evasion.

FARNSWORTH: All right, maybe that generation let things go by the boards, but there were still values hanging in the air while we were growing up. Values which were drummed into us at those posh private schools they could still afford to send us to, and at those Ivy League colleges that still accepted us as legacies, and even at those long cocktail hours and family *parties?* dinners that still went on—whenever our parents could find people to cook and serve.

MRS FARNSWORTH: I hated those things. I made a point of not listening to anything that was said.

FARNSWORTH: You listened to your grandmother.

MRS FARNSWORTH: All right. Yes. Her.

*cut?* FARNSWORTH: And now you sense her shaking her head over every word you try to write ~~in your book~~.

MRS FARNSWORTH: I sense her saying, "You go, girl," that's what I sense.

*cut?* FARNSWORTH: No, that's what her cook ~~in the kitchen~~ might say. But your grandmother? Never! She's saying, "Don't point, Margery! Particularly at presidents." She's saying, "Don't tell tales out of school." She's *odd* saying, "You lost the man thirty years ago, so stop whining and being a poor sport." And she's saying, "Stop making disparaging remarks about a nice boy from a good family who has no possible chance to answer back." Isn't that what you hear your *?* grandmother saying, Marjorie?

MRS FARNSWORTH: Only in the background.

*even?* FARNSWORTH: And if you and your academic amanuensis here manage to drown her out, and produce your book, and get your name in the paper— which you would, immediately—wouldn't your grandmother ~~also~~ say that you've become cheap and vulgar and embarrass~~ing~~ *an?* *ment* to your family and friends?

MRS FARNSWORTH: She'd say it. I wouldn't.

FARNSWORTH: Then what about that first paragraph of yours? The one I like so much. Isn't it all about trust? Trust in a society that doesn't steal ski parkas? Trust in a world that doesn't kiss and tell? How ~~can~~ could you go on to write a book which contradicts all that?

MRS FARNSWORTH: Because I happen to feel...I happen to—

FARNSWORTH: You can't do it, darling. It goes completely against your grain. And all the psychiatrists and writing courses in the world won't ever get you past that fine first paragraph. You can't go on to violate your own soul.

MRS FARNSWORTH: Oh stop...stop...

FARNSWORTH: And I'll tell you something else.

MRS FARNSWORTH: I don't want to hear anything else.

FARNSWORTH: I know why you're so angry with Bush in the first place.

MRS FARNSWORTH: Because he's a crummy president, that's why.

FARNSWORTH: That's not it, and you know it.

JANET: *(From the audience)* I know why. She's angry with him because he betrayed her. Hell hath no fury like a woman scorned.

AMY: *(From audience)* Especially when the guy he goes on to become president.

FARNSWORTH: I'm sorry, but that's not it either. *(To MRS FARNSWORTH)* You're angry with him because he's doing ~~everything~~ the very thing you can't bring yourself to do. ~~He's~~ betraying his class.

MRS FARNSWORTH: Oh please, oh please.

FARNSWORTH: Think about it. Over the years, he has rejected everything you were told was important. He doesn't read, he can't sing a note, and he hates to travel. What's more, his tennis is terrible and his bridge game worse. And he has topped it all off by putting on a ten-gallon hat and a fake Texas accent, and pretending he wasn't one of us in the first place.

AMY: *(From audience)* That's one thing I give him credit for. He sensed the Titanic was sinking, and jumped to the Southwest.

MRS FARNSWORTH: Yes, but he didn't even land on a horse. The man can't ride, not even with a Western saddle. All he does is wander around that so-called ranch, taking swipes at scrub oaks with a chain saw.

FARNSWORTH: See! There it is! She's a class-conscious snob after all!

MRS FARNSWORTH: O K, O K. O K! Enough said!

FARNSWORTH: Then forget that book.

GORDON: I'm still not clear what values she'd be betraying.

FARNSWORTH: I'll spell them out on the blackboard, if I may. *(Goes to the blackboard, starts writing: "CIVILITY" "CHARITY" "RESPONSIBILITY". He stands back and looks at them, then crosses them out.)* No, no. This is wrong. It looks boastful and self-congratulatory. So how do we describe what I'm talking about? We can't. But we know it when we see it.

GORDON: That's what the Supreme Court said about pornography.

FARNSWORTH: Yes. All right. Why not?

MRS FARNSWORTH: May I say something else about pornography?

FARNSWORTH: I wouldn't, darling.

MRS FARNSWORTH: I want to. I hear that George Bush makes everyone pray before meetings and say grace at meals and stuff like that. Now that to me is pornographic. My grandmother used to say that religion, like sex, is a private thing. The more public it becomes, the more embarrassing.

AMY: *(From audience)* But religion helped him give up liquor.

MRS FARNSWORTH: Maybe it did. All right. Fine. Any port in a storm, say I. But that doesn't mean he should throw it in our face. Religion, I mean. Not liquor. Though I don't believe in throwing around good alcohol.. Even though I don't drink anymore. Oh now I'm all mixed up. Shit.

FARNSWORTH: That's all right, darling. *(To audience)* You see? She's thoroughly confused, but her sturdy WASP values still shine through. Except for that slight slip into vulgarity at the very end.

MRS FARNSWORTH: Just stop, Forrest. Please. I beg you. Stop.

FARNSWORTH: All right. Let me just conclude the discussion by saying that we're stuck with a president who's way over his head. And why? Because he's been in bailed out and propped up by his family all of his life. Which is why he is now so dependent on a bunch of ruthless Republicans who are manipulating him for their own fell purposes.

GORDON: You're sounding a little like a Democrat, Mr Farnsworth.

FARNSWORTH: That's because I haven't supported a Republican since Eisenhower. Nixon? No. Reagan? '56 Get serious. Even Papa Bush. Couldn't do it.

MRS FARNSWORTH: Now he tells me.

FARNSWORTH: Thank God for the secret ballot.

GORDON: Why didn't you tell your wife?

FARNSWORTH: Because I believe in the two party system. Especially in marriage. It keeps you both honest. Can you imagine how boring we'd be if we sat around agreeing with each other? Don't you hate couples who do that? We liked this, we hated that. We, we, we, all the way home.

MRS FARNSWORTH: Then go home by yourself, Forrest. I'll make this book anonymous, like that little man who did the hatchet job on Clinton.

MR FARNSWORTH: It won't work, darling. You'd just feel sneaky and mean. Besides, if the only way we can pry the poor soul out of office is by publishing some unsubstantiated account of his youthful transgressions, then maybe he deserves to stay on.

GORDON: What? Never! Stick with it, Mrs Farnsworth!

MRS FARNSWORTH: I'm not sure I can, now. He's pulled the rug completely out from under me.

FARNSWORTH: It was a nice rug, dear, but wrong for the room.

MRS FARNSWORTH: That's a clever way of putting it. Except I feel like a fool. (She goes upstage.)

GORDON: (To FARNSWORTH) What do you propose we do about Bush, then, Mr Farnsworth?

FARNSWORTH: We work for an articulate, electable opposition. We insist on an intelligent airing of the issues. And we hope and trust that a majority of the American people will sense the chap's inadequacy, and send him back to his baseball team.

GORDON: A majority tried to do that in 2000, and he still got in.

FARNSWORTH: Then we work for a larger majority this time out. The point is to judge the man on what he is doing now, rather than on what he may or may not have done in the past.

GORDON: And if we lose?

FARNSWORTH: Then we try harder the next election. Meanwhile let's not go overboard here. The poor lad is frightened enough as it is. Those beady little eyes darting nervously from teleprompter to teleprompter. That sad little strut as he hurries to his helicopter. There's nothing more dangerous than a man who's out of his league and beginning to realize it. Am I right, darling?

MRS FARNSWORTH: *(From upstage)* Don't ask me. You've broken my spirit.

FARNSWORTH: Oh please, sweetheart. Stop sulking.

MRS FARNSWORTH: Why shouldn't I sulk? You've taken all the wind out of my sails, I feel I've totally run out steam.

FARNSWORTH: *(To* GORDON*)* Don't you love these old WASP expressions? They come from the shipping and railroad industries.

MRS FARNSWORTH: I'm tempted to give you the finger, Forrest.

FARNSWORTH: Uh-oh. *(Low to* GORDON*)* I believe she may be sliding into one of her lows. It's time we went home. *(Shakes hands)* Goodbye, professor.

GORDON: I'm not a professor.

FARNSWORTH: Maybe some day you will be.

GORDON: I don't want to be. I'm a writer.

FARNSWORTH: Ah well. Then let me suggest that you write things that are amusing and entertaining. Add some suspense and military history, and you're sure to succeed. *(To* MRS FARNSWORTH*)* Let's go, darling. Let's demonstrate another sturdy WASP value, by saying a brisk and snappy goodbye.

MRS FARNSWORTH: I won't go till the class is over.

FARNSWORTH: It's over now, isn't it, Professor?

GORDON: No. *(Glancing at his watch)* We still have a little time.

MRS FARNSWORTH: Good, because I need some sense of... *(To* GORDON*)* What's that word we talked about?

GORDON: Closure.

MRS FARNSWORTH: Thank you. *(To* FARNSWORTH*)* I'm looking for closure, Forrest.

FARNSWORTH: Darling...

MRS FARNSWORTH: Wait for me in the car, please.

FARNSWORTH: I'll give you five minutes. *(He looks at his watch.)* And then, if you don't show up, I'll have to... I'll have to ...Well, I'll have to do something, won't I? Meanwhile... *(To audience)* Goodbye, all. Keep an eye on her, please. She's my most precious possession. *(He goes.)*

*(Pause)*

MRS FARNSWORTH: *(To class)* See what I'm up against? "Possession." *(To* GORDON*)* I suppose I should resign from this course.

GORDON: Resign? Why?

MRS FARNSWORTH: Because I have nothing to write about.

GORDON: You won't write about Bush?

MRS FARNSWORTH: I just can't. My husband wins this round. Bush just makes me angry and resentful. That's nothing to build a book on.

GORDON: Some of the best writing comes out of anger and resentment.

MRS FARNSWORTH: Not from me.

GORDON: Shit.

MRS FARNSWORTH: I'm sorry, but that's the way I feel. I also feel very embarrassed. I sign up for your course, ask to go first, commandeer the whole evening, and end up with nothing on my plate. That's why I'd better resign. Do I get a rebate on my tuition?

GORDON: No.

MRS FARNSWORTH: Darn it.

GORDON: And I won't accept your resignation anyway. I want you to start over. Go back to your first paragraph.

MRS FARNSWORTH: Skiing in the sixties? That was too nostalgic. And didn't it seem a little snooty?

GORDON: Snooty?

MRS FARNSWORTH: It sort of said "We ski and you don't". Didn't you feel that?

GORDON: All right. Yes. It was a little exclusionary

MRS FARNSWORTH: I don't want to be exclusionary any more. All that talk from Forrest about WASP values was too...what? ...Too tribal, wasn't it? Sure it was.

GORDON: Nothing wrong with writing about your roots. For example, I'm basing my own book on my grandfather who came over from Odessa and—

MRS FARNSWORTH: Stop! I don't want to hear. Why do we always have to frame people as Jews, or WASPs, or whatever? Why do we always have to carry that ethnic or social junk around on our backs? ...You've got a little cut on your cheek, by the way..

GORDON: From shaving before class.

MRS FARNSWORTH: Interesting...

GORDON: Interesting?

MRS FARNSWORTH: Because it's so...specific. Isn't it strange? Here I've been yacking away all evening about all these supposedly important things, and only now am I really seeing you. Tell me something about yourself.

GORDON: Me?

MRS FARNSWORTH: Something interesting about your life. Besides your grandfather.

GORDON: Oh well I'm ...Forget it.

MRS FARNSWORTH: Come on. I've reeled off all this stuff about me. Your turn now.

GORDON: *(To audience)* This is somewhat embarrassing...

MRS FARNSWORTH: Go ahead.

STUDENTS: Come on... Tell us... Why not?

GORDON: I happen to be the runner-up table-tennis champion for the tri-state area.

MRS FARNSWORTH: No kidding!

GORDON: I am.

STUDENTS: Cool! ...Way to go! ...That is sooo interesting!

MRS FARNSWORTH: You look like a lovely athlete.

GORDON: Thanks.

MRS FARNSWORTH: You should write about that in your book. Maybe it will give you closure.

GORDON: I 'm not sure that the Jewish experience in America should culminate in a ping-pong game.

MRS FARNSWORTH: You care about ping pong, don't you?

GORDON: Too much, maybe, these days.

MRS FARNSWORTH: Nonsense. Strike while the iron's hot. *(To class)* I'll bet everyone here has something crucial to write about.. *(To GORDON)* Let's ask the ones who've been talking. Could we get them up here, please?

GORDON: O K. *(Calling out)* Amy Needleman...Rick... and...I forget your name.

JANET: *(From audience)* Janet.

GORDON: Come up here, guys.

*(STUDENTS come onto the stage awkwardly.)*

They're all yours.

MRS FARNSWORTH: We'll start with you, Amy, because I grabbed your turn. Tell us what really interests you.

GORDON: Besides your cat.

MRS FARNSWORTH: No. The cat counts. If it's important to her.

AMY: It is. Very.

MRS FARNSWORTH: Then it's worth writing about. You've been on the right track all along, Amy

AMY: I know it.

MRS FARNSWORTH: What about you, Rick? And I hope you won't tell us you're gay.

RICK: I am.

MRS FARNSWORTH: Oh Lord. Here we go again.

RICK: That's not what I want to write about, though.

MRS FARNSWORTH: Thank God.

RICK: I've got an autistic younger brother. He sees the world in a very different way. I want to get into his head and write my way out.

MRS FARNSWORTH: That sounds absolutely fascinating ...How about you, Janet?

JANET: I'm getting married in July.

MRS FARNSWORTH: Wonderful!

JANET: To a boy who's two and a half years younger than I am.

MRS FARNSWORTH: More wonderful.

JANET: He's small and brown and comes from Kuala-Lumpur.

MRS FARNSWORTH: Sounds yummy.

JANET: I want to write something very sexy..

MRS FARNSWORTH: Can't wait. *(To* GORDON*)* You see? Everyone here has a story.

GORDON: But you've got the best story of all.

MRS FARNSWORTH: Nope. I'm a woman without a story now. It's back to New Canaan for me.

GORDON: Oh come on, Mrs Farnsworth. You must have other things to tell.

MRS FARNSWORTH: I'll tell you one thing. I don't like being called "Mrs Farnsworth" any more. Your first name is Gordon, isn't it? I know that from your poem in *The Nation*.

GORDON: Right.

MRS FARNSWORTH: I'll call you Gordon.

GORDON: Wish you would.

MRS FARNSWORTH: And you can call me Margery...

GORDON: What? Without kissing you?

MRS FARNSWORTH: You can kiss me goodbye.

GORDON: *(He gives her a sweet kiss on the cheek)* Goodbye, Margery.

MRS FARNSWORTH: Thanks. I needed that.

GORDON: The kiss?

MRS FARNSWORTH: The first name. At least it means I'm not just somebody's wife.

GORDON: You're Margery Farnsworth.

MRS FARNSWORTH: Except that makes me sound as if I went to Miss Porter's School, in Farmington, Connecticut. *(Pause)* Which I did. *(Getting her coat)* How about Marge? Call me Marge. Like I'm working in a diner.

.GORDON: Think your grandmother would approve?

MRS FARNSWORTH: My grandmother's dead, Gordon.

GORDON: May she rest in peace.

MRS FARNSWORTH: *(As she fusses in her bag, puts on lipstick)* Here comes a little speech. Maybe if Bush— oh Lord, here I go talking about Bush again—but maybe if we *all* could learn to look at people not as good or evil, or Republicans or terrorists, but simply as fellow human beings with different first names, things might improve in this country.

RICK: And in the rest of the world.

MRS FARNSWORTH: Yes, because we're all valuable in and of ourselves, aren't we? Aren't we?

GORDON: We are, Marge. So write about that, and come back next week..

MRS FARNSWORTH: Oh no. If I wrote that down, it would just sound sappy.

*15*

(FARNSWORTH *reappears in the aisle.*)

FARNSWORTH: Excuse me, but the police are down below.

GORDON, MRS FARNSWORTH, & STUDENTS: *(Together)* The police?

MRS FARNSWORTH: *(To* GORDON*)* They must have found out I was spilling the beans.

GORDON: *(To* FARNSWORTH*)* I hope they realize there's still freedom of speech in this country.

FARNSWORTH: I hope they do, too, but that's not the issue. They say we're illegally parked, so they're giving us a ticket.

GORDON: Did you tell them your wife was a student here?

FARNSWORTH: I did. And I added that she had injured her ankle, so I needed to drive her home.

MRS FARNSWORTH: I'll bet they didn't buy that one.

FARNSWORTH: No actually they did, darling. And they said if I produced you immediately, they'd tear up the ticket. Which will save us at least one hundred and fifty dollars.

MRS FARNSWORTH: *(To* GORDON*)* I'd better go.

FARNSWORTH: There's another WASP value. We're very careful about money.

MRS FARNSWORTH: That's not the reason I'm going, but I'll let him think it. *(She takes* FARNSWORTH's *arm.)*

GORDON: Will you be back next week?

FARNSWORTH: I think not.

MRS FARNSWORTH: Unless I can write something.

FARNSWORTH: Not about Bush, please..

MRS FARNSWORTH: Oh, I'm way beyond Bush.

FARNSWORTH: Delighted to hear it, darling.

GORDON: *(Calling after her)* Just bring in a paragraph.
A thought. An incomplete sentence.

FARNSWORTH: I don't like incomplete sentences.

MRS FARNSWORTH: *(To* GORDON*)* I might write just a
tiny little sketch.

GORDON: Do it.

FARNSWORTH: On what subject, dear?

MRS FARNSWORTH: I'm suddenly thinking about John
Kerry.

FARNSWORTH: You don't even know John Kerry, dear.

MRS FARNSWORTH: I spent an entire football weekend
with him at Yale, that's all.

FARNSWORTH: *(To audience)* She's just doing this to get
my goat.

MRS FARNSWORTH: Goodbye, Amy, Rick, and Janet.

STUDENTS: Goodbye, Marge.

MRS FARNSWORTH: Goodbye, Gordon.

GORDON: Goodbye, Marge.

FARNSWORTH: *(As they start off)* Marge? Is it Marge now?

MRS FARNSWORTH: For some people it is.

FARNSWORTH: Next you'll say John Kerry called you
that.

MRS FARNSWORTH: No. Actually he called me
sweetheart.

FARNSWORTH: *(To audience)* She's teasing, of course.
*(To* MRS FARNSWORTH, *as they go)* What would you
say about John Kerry, dear?

MRS FARNSWORTH: I'll start by saying he's a perfectly marvelous man.

*(They go out; we hear them arguing offstage)*

*(*GORDON *watches them go, then goes quickly to the board, then writes "MARGE", circles it, and "Save!!!" next to it)*

GORDON: *(To student and audience)* And that's enough about writing for one evening. Next week, Amy, we'll deal with your cat.... Goodnight all.

*(Slow blackout)*

## END OF PLAY